RIVERS AND STREAMS

Rebecca Siegel

Illustrated by Tom Casteel

Titles in the **Explore Waterways** Set

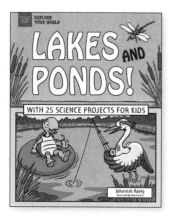

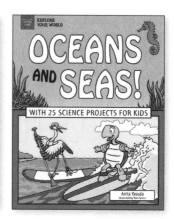

Check out more titles at www.nomadpress.net

Nomad Press
A division of Nomad Communications
10 9 8 7 6 5 4 3 2 1

This book was manufactured by Versa Press,
East Peoria, Illinois
November 2018, Job #J18-09190

ISBN Softcover: 978-1-61930-704-9
ISBN Hardcover: 978-1-61930-702-5

Educational Consultant, Marla Conn

Questions regarding the ordering of this book should be addressed to
Nomad Press
2456 Christian St.
White River Junction, VT 05001
www.nomadpress.net

CONTENTS

Interested in primary sources? Look for this icon. Use a smartphone or tablet app to scan the QR code and explore more! Photos are also primary sources because a photograph takes a picture at the moment something happens.

You can find a list of URLs on the Resources page. If the QR code doesn't work, try searching the internet with the Keyword Prompts to find other helpful sources.

KEYWORD PROMPTS

rivers and streams 🔍

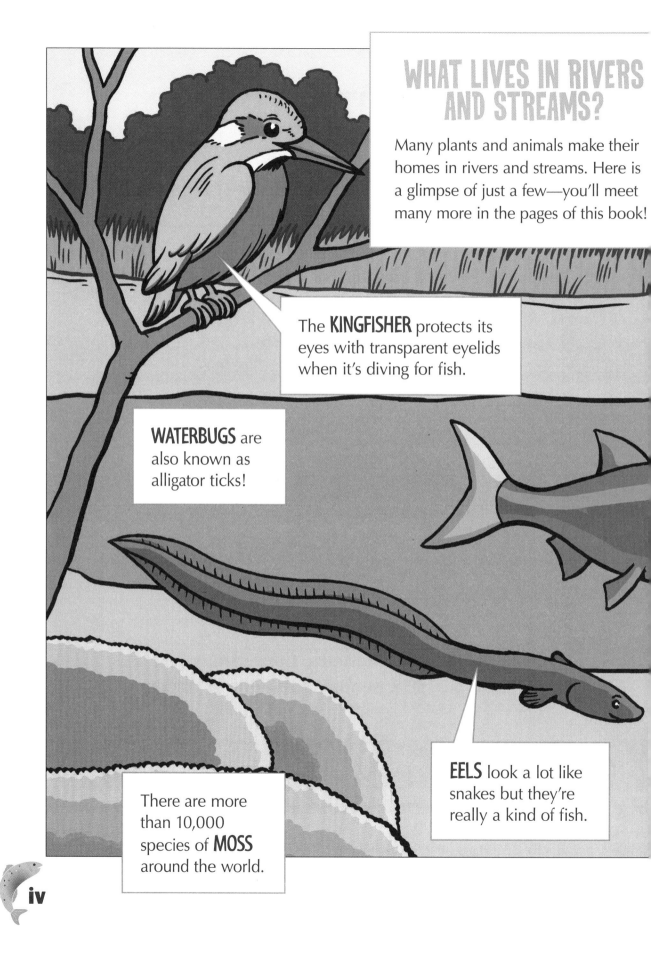

WHAT LIVES IN RIVERS AND STREAMS?

Many plants and animals make their homes in rivers and streams. Here is a glimpse of just a few—you'll meet many more in the pages of this book!

The **KINGFISHER** protects its eyes with transparent eyelids when it's diving for fish.

WATERBUGS are also known as alligator ticks!

EELS look a lot like snakes but they're really a kind of fish.

There are more than 10,000 species of **MOSS** around the world.

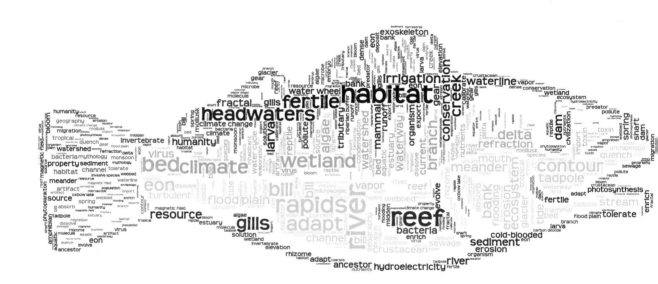

INTRODUCTION

WHAT ARE RIVERS AND STREAMS?

There are more than 165 major rivers on our planet, plus thousands of smaller rivers and streams! The chances are good that you've been near or on a river sometime in your life!

What did you notice about the river? How would you describe it? When you are near a river, what does it smell like? What does it look like? What are some of the characteristics of rivers and streams?

WORDS TO KNOW

river: a large quantity of water that flows through a channel from its source to its mouth.

stream: a narrow flow of water that has a current that runs in one direction. A river is a type of stream.

1

RIVERS AND STREAMS!

current: the movement of the water in a body of water. In rivers and streams, the current moves in one direction: downhill toward the ocean.

WORDS ⊙ KNOW

Rivers form naturally and contain fresh water. They are longer than they are wide and flow toward a larger body of water. A stream is any narrow flow of water that has a current that runs in one direction. In fact, a stream is simply a smaller river. Let's take a look at the different parts of a river.

THE PARTS OF A RIVER

It's easy to think of a river as just one thing, the way you might think of a human being as one thing or a building as one thing. But if you look more closely, you'll find that a river, like a human or a building, is made of many different parts.

One way to look at the parts of a human is from top to bottom. A human has a head, a neck, a torso, arms, hands, legs, and feet. If you look more closely at the head, you'll see that it has hair, eyebrows, eyes, ears, a nose, a mouth, and a chin.

Look closely at an eye and you'll see that it has a cornea, pupil, iris, lid, and eyelashes. If you had a microscope, you could see even smaller parts!

The same is true of a river or stream. Bodies of water have lots of different parts.

DID YOU KNOW?

The Mississippi River is about 2,300 miles long. Its narrowest point, just 20 to 30 feet wide, is at Lake Itasca in Minnesota. It's widest point, at 11 miles wide, is Lake Winnibigoshish, also in Minnesota.

The **source** of a river, also called its **headwaters**, is where the river starts. If you think of a river as a long, straight racetrack, the source is where the river's race begins. A river's source might be a **spring** or melting snow in the mountains.

The end of a river is where it crosses its finish line. Called the river's **mouth**, it is the place where it empties into a larger body of water, such as a lake, the ocean, or even another river. The **channel** is the river or stream's path, from its source to its mouth. Part of a river channel is the water itself.

The channel has two other important parts—the **bed** and the **bank**.

source: where a river or stream starts.

headwaters: the source of a river or stream.

spring: a place where water from underground flows up to the earth's surface.

mouth: the end of a river. The mouth is where the river joins a larger body of water, such as a lake or ocean.

channel: a river or stream's path.

bed: the ground that a river flows over, including the land at the bottom of the river and the sides up to the river's waterline.

bank: the land on the edge of a body of water. Riverbanks are the land on either side of the river's channel.

WORDS ⊕ KNOW

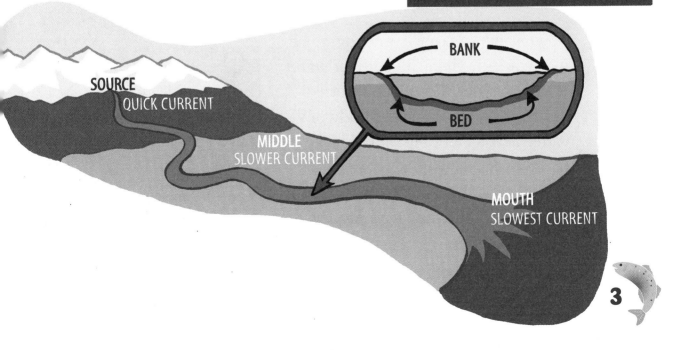

SOURCE
QUICK CURRENT

MIDDLE
SLOWER CURRENT

BANK

BED

MOUTH
SLOWEST CURRENT

3

RIVERS AND STREAMS!

A river's bed is all of the land that cradles the river, from the very bottom of the deepest part of the river all the way up to the river's **waterline**. The banks are the land on each side of the river that is above the waterline.

A river's path usually changes in several ways as it winds from source to mouth. At its source, the water is often flowing quickly and is **turbulent**. The river's channel is usually narrow, and its path is pretty straight.

Toward the middle of a river, it becomes wider and deeper. The water moves more slowly. Its path may wander, following a winding, S-curve path called a **meander**. Finally, as the river reaches its mouth, it is at its slowest and widest.

Sometimes a river is moving much more quickly than the body of water it empties into. The place where the river meets the other body of water acts as a brake on the river. If the river has been carrying a lot of **sediment**, this sudden change in speed can make the river **deposit** its load of sediment.

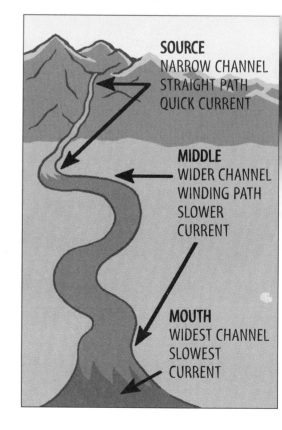

SOURCE
NARROW CHANNEL
STRAIGHT PATH
QUICK CURRENT

MIDDLE
WIDER CHANNEL
WINDING PATH
SLOWER CURRENT

MOUTH
WIDEST CHANNEL
SLOWEST CURRENT

As time passes, this deposited sediment builds up. It forms new land in the mouth of the river, called a **delta**.

RIVER COMPARISONS

Now that we know some of the **properties** of a river, let's take a look at how rivers are different from other **waterways**.

A **creek** or a brook is a stream. Different regions have different names for streams, including crick, falls, burn, and many more! A **tributary** or **branch** is a part of a river that stems off from the main river. These are usually smaller than rivers but larger than creeks or brooks.

delta: land that forms from the buildup of sediment carried by a river to its mouth.

property: a characteristic, quality, or distinctive feature of something.

waterway: a channel or body of water.

creek: a small stream, also called a brook. The word you use for this depends on where you live. For example, some people call a small stream a creek, a kill, or a run.

tributary: a river or stream that flows into a larger river or lake.

branch: a stream that flows away from the main stem of a river.

WORDS ᴛᴏ KNOW

A RIVER DELTA

CREDIT: NOAA FISHERIES

RIVERS AND STREAMS!

Think about the ocean. What does it look and smell like? How is this different from the sights and smells of a river?

For one thing, the shape of a river is different from the shape of an ocean or lake. Most rivers are long and narrow. Remember, a river is always longer than it is wide. Even the Mississippi River, which can be so wide in places that it actually forms a lake, is much longer than it is wide.

Another way that rivers are different from oceans is the way they move. You probably know that oceans have **tides**. Tides move through an ocean in a regular pattern, pushing the water in one direction, then pulling it back in the other direction.

ANNUAL FLOODING

Flooding is when the water in a river rises over its banks and onto land that is normally dry. Some flooding happens because of storms or unusual weather patterns. Flooding can also be an annual event, part of the river's normal cycle. For example, the Nile River in Egypt floods every year because of the yearly **monsoons.** Egyptians celebrate this annual flood in a two-week holiday called Wafaa El-Nil.

You can watch a video about the Nile's famous flood at this website.

KEYWORD PROMPTS

Nile PBS video

elevation: the height of something above sea level.

WORDS TO KNOW

Unlike oceans, a river's water usually moves in only direction, pulled downhill by gravity from the river's start to its end. This flow of water in one direction is called the river's current. The current in a river almost always flows toward the ocean or to a lake that the river feeds.

Can you think of another difference between a river and an ocean? Think of the type of water in an ocean. You wouldn't want to drink it! Oceans contain salt water. Rivers and lakes contain fresh water.

WHERE DO RIVER TROUT KEEP THEIR MONEY?

A river bank!

Inlets and canals are other narrow bodies of water that are similar to rivers. Like rivers, inlets are longer than they are wide. Inlets are always connected to oceans, while some rivers are connected to oceans and some are not.

Canals are different from rivers because they are made by humans. Canals are formed by digging a channel between two bodies of water that are at slightly different elevations from each other. The difference in elevation allows the water to flow from the higher body of water to the lower body of water.

DID YOU KNOW?

A river delta is called a delta because it looks somewhat like the fourth letter of the Greek alphabet: Delta △

tropical: the hot climate zone to the north and south of the equator.

climate: the average weather patterns in an area during a long period of time.

equator: the imaginary line around the earth, halfway between the North and South Poles.

WORDS TO KNOW

DID YOU KNOW?

The tropical climate of Panama was a major problem for early engineers and builders who worked on the Panama Canal in the nineteenth century. Thousands of workers died from snake and insect bites and tropical diseases such as malaria and yellow fever!

Have you heard of the Panama Canal? This famous canal connects the Atlantic Ocean with the Pacific Ocean through Panama, a country just north of South America near the **equator.** Construction on the Panama Canal was begun in 1881, but the project wasn't finished until 1914!

PANAMA CANAL

WATERSHEDS

Rivers are actually collections of smaller waterways. As they meander through the land, they pick up other rivers and streams along their travels. When one downward flowing stream meets another one, they join together.

An area of land where all the water above and below ground collects and drains into the same body of water is called a **watershed**.

In a watershed, rainwater or snowmelt collects together and is funneled toward the same drainage point. When rivers from neighboring watersheds join each other, they create even bigger rivers. Eventually, all of the rivers in all of the connected watersheds empty into one drainage point—an ocean.

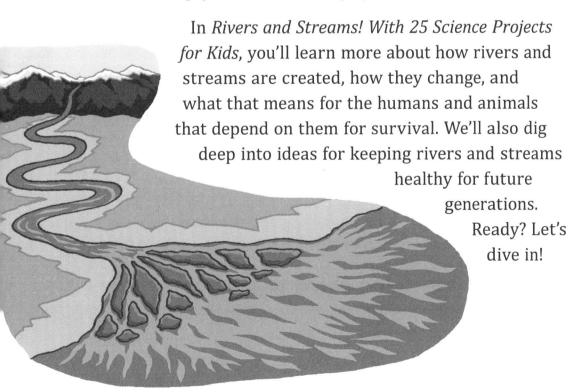

In *Rivers and Streams! With 25 Science Projects for Kids*, you'll learn more about how rivers and streams are created, how they change, and what that means for the humans and animals that depend on them for survival. We'll also dig deep into ideas for keeping rivers and streams healthy for future generations.

Ready? Let's dive in!

9

GOOD SCIENCE PRACTICES

Every good scientist keeps a science journal. In the first activity, you'll make a notebook to use as your science journal. Write down your ideas, observations, and comparisons as you read this book.

For many projects in this book, make and use a scientific method worksheet, like the one shown here. Scientists use the scientific method to keep their experiments organized. A scientific method worksheet will help you keep track of your observations and results.

Each chapter of this book begins with a question to help guide your exploration of rivers and streams.

Scientific Method Worksheet
Question: What problem are we trying to solve?
Research: What information is already known?
Hypothesis/Prediction: What do I think the answer will be?
Equipment: What supplies do I need?
Method: What steps will I follow?
Results: What happened and why?

? INVESTIGATE!

How would you describe a river to someone who has never seen one before?

Keep the question in your mind as you read the chapter. Record your thoughts, questions, and observations in your science journal. At the end of each chapter, use your science journal to think of answers to the question. Does your answer change as you read the chapter?

RIVER SCIENCE JOURNAL

Make a science journal so that you can record everything you learn about rivers!

SUPPLIES

* 2 pieces of cardstock, 8½ by 11 inches
* 25–30 sheets of blank paper, 8½ by 11 inches
* 3-hole punch
* piece of ribbon or string about 1 foot long
* scissors
* colored pens, markers, and other art supplies

1 Use the 3-hole punch to make three evenly spaced holes along the long left edge of the paper and cardstock. You will probably be able to do a few at a time.

2 Put the sheets of blank paper between the two pieces of cardstock, lining up the holes.

3 Cut the ribbon or string into three equal pieces, each about 3 to 4 inches long. Thread one piece of ribbon or string through a hole, making sure it goes through all of the sheets of paper and cardstock.

4 Tie a knot or a double bow. Tie it tight enough so that the paper doesn't slip around too much, but not so tight that you tear the paper or can't open the journal.

5 Do the same thing with the other two pieces of ribbon or string and the remaining two holes.

6 Use your markers and art supplies to decorate the front and back covers. Don't forget to write "River Science Journal" on the front cover!

RIVER WATCHING

SUPPLIES

✳ science journal and pencil

✳ river or stream

✳ small jars or containers with lids

Observing things closely is an important part of being a scientist. In this activity, you'll watch a river to see what you can notice about it. If you don't have a river or stream nearby, you can ask an adult for help finding a video of a river or stream on the Internet.

> **Caution:** Always have an adult with you when you are near any kind of water, including rivers and streams.

1 Before visiting a river or stream, imagine what it will be like. What will you see, hear, feel, and smell? In your journal, write "Imaginary River" and then write or draw a description.

2 Now go to a river or stream or watch a video. On the back of the page where you described the imaginary river, write "Real River."

3 Look at the river. What do you see? In what direction is the water flowing? How quickly is it flowing? Is there anything in the water, such as rocks, branches, a waterfall, or a beaver dam? Do you see any animals, fish, or birds? Write down your observations.

4 Listen to the river. What do you hear? Is the water making a lot of noise or is it very quiet? Do you hear any birds or other animal sounds? Write down what you hear.

5 Notice the air around you and the river. Touch the water. Does the air feel cool or warm? How about the water? Do you smell anything? Write down what you feel and smell.

6 Look at the land on the sides the river. Do you see rocks, soil, or plants? Do you see human-made walls? Do you see sand or gravel? Write down what you see.

7 Compare the description of your imaginary river with the description of the real river. What did you notice through your observation that you didn't imagine?

THINK ABOUT IT! Collect some river water in your containers to use in future projects. Can you see anything floating in your water?

TRY THIS! One way to learn more about how the parts of a river work together is by making your own river! Using modeling clay, tinfoil, mud, or other material, form the shape of a river in a long container. Can you name all the parts of your river? What can you add to the banks to make it more realistic? Add water to your river and find a way to create a current, whether it's by tipping your container to create a slope or something else. How does the water behave in your river? Is it similar to the way the water behaved in the real river you observed?

CRUMPLED PAPER WATERSHED

Large watersheds are difficult to see because they are all around us and we are small compared with mountains, hills, and valleys. One way to see how a large watershed works is to make your own.

SUPPLIES

* plain paper, 8½ by 11 inches
* spray bottle filled with plain water
* blue and brown or black water-based markers
* science journal and pencil

1 Crumple up the sheet of paper into a loose ball, then open the ball and smooth it out most of the way. It should still have bumps and ridges on it. Think of this bumpy paper as a piece of land. Use the brown or black marker to gently color the tops of the mountains and ridges. Use the blue marker to draw where you think the rivers and lakes are in the valleys.

2 On a new page in your journal, start a scientific method worksheet. What will happen when you spray water on your watershed?

3 Put the paper on a washable surface or in the bathtub, then use the spray bottle to "rain" over your land. At first, spray gently to make a mist of water and see what happens. Try spraying more water. What happens if you put your watershed on a slope?

4 Record your observations your journal. Were your predictions accurate? If not, why not? What can you conclude from your experiment?

THINK ABOUT IT! In your watershed, where would you get drinking water? Where would it be good to farm? Where would there be a danger of flooding?

CHAPTER 1

WHY RIVERS AND STREAMS ARE IMPORTANT

You know that rivers and streams provide fresh water—but so do lakes and ponds! Why are rivers and streams important to the planet?

Rivers and streams are important for many reasons. They are part of the **water cycle** and they provide **habitats** for many animals and plants. They are also an important **resource** for humans.

WORDS ⊤⊚ KNOW

water cycle: the continuous movement of water from the earth to the clouds and back again.

habitat: an area where certain plants and animals live together.

resource: something that people can use.

15

THE WATER CYCLE

All the water on Earth is all the water that has ever existed here. Water is continually being recycled through a process called the water cycle. This means the water you drink today was around when dinosaurs were alive!

INVESTIGATE!

What would the world be like without rivers and streams?

WHAT DID ONE RAINDROP SAY TO THE OTHER?

Two's company. Three's a cloud!

You can think of the water cycle as a big wheel that rolls across the land, picking up water from the earth, lifting it up into the sky, and then dropping it back down to the land again. Sometimes, the water is liquid, sometimes it's frozen solid as ice, and sometimes it's in the air as a gas.

CITY ON A RIVER

Venice, Italy, is a city built on an **archipelago** of 118 islands that lie between the mouths of the Po and the Piave Rivers. To get around on foot, by horse, or by cart, the Venetians built bridges from island to island. The roads in Venice are narrow and wind around the old buildings and walls. Today, there's no room for cars or buses. So how to the people in Venice get around? By water! Water buses are one of the primary modes of transportation in Venice, speeding commuters from island to island.

DID YOU KNOW?

If you collected and measured all the water in the oceans, lakes, rivers, and ponds, as well as under the land's surface, you would have about 326 million trillion gallons. That's enough to fill 410 trillion Olympic-sized swimming pools!

evaporation: the process by which a liquid becomes a gas.

condensation: when water vapor turns into a liquid.

precipitation: the falling to the earth of rain, snow, or any form of water.

molecule: a group of atoms, which are the smallest particles of matter.

vapor: a gas.

WORDS TO KNOW

The water cycle is made up of three processes: evaporation, condensation, and precipitation.

When a liquid is heated enough, the molecules in the liquid start to move quickly. When molecules move quickly enough, they escape into the air as vapor. This process of liquid turning into a vapor, or a gas, is called evaporation.

Have you ever noticed that a puddle in the road disappears after a while? That's evaporation in action! The heat of the sun evaporates water from puddles, rivers, lakes—any body of water.

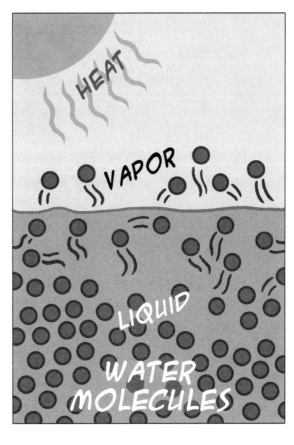

RIVERS AND STREAMS!

Once the water is up in the air, how does it come back down? The water vapor in the air cools. As it cools, it changes from a vapor back to tiny drops of liquid water.

This process is called condensation. When these tiny drops clump together, they form clouds. When the clouds release their gathered water, we get precipitation in the form of rain or snow. The whole process starts over again when that water evaporates back into the air.

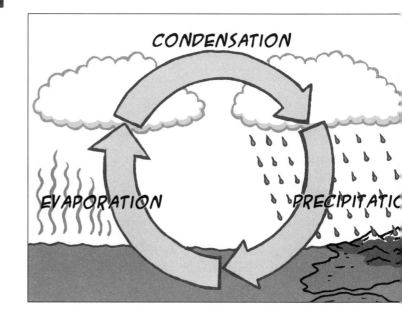

RIVERS ARE HOMES

Many **organisms** make their homes in rivers. The animals, plants, and other organisms, along with the water they live in, form an **ecosystem**. An ecosystem includes the organisms that live in an environment and all the parts of that environment, including the water, the soil, and the rocks.

If one part of an ecosystem changes, all the other parts are affected. Can you think of some ecosystems where you live?

Many river **inhabitants** are quite small. Some are even **microscopic**. The smallest organisms that call a river home are **bacteria**, which are single-celled organisms. Other tiny river organisms include some types of **algae**, which are very small, free-floating plants. You'll learn more about the animals that live in rivers and streams in Chapter 3.

inhabitant: a person, animal, or other organism that lives in a particular place.

microscopic: something so small it can be seen only with a microscope.

bacteria: tiny organisms that live in animals, plants, soil, and water. Some bacteria are helpful and some are harmful.

algae: a plant-like organism that lives in water and grows by converting energy from the sun into food.

irrigation: the process of delivering water to plants or fields where crops are planted.

WORDS TO KNOW

WATER

Rivers are important to another animal you know pretty well—humans! In fact, it's difficult to image human life without rivers and streams.

Like other animals, humans have always depended on rivers and streams for fresh water. Long before we invented faucets, showers, and garden sprinklers, we got our water for drinking, cooking, washing, and **irrigation** from rivers and other freshwater sources.

RIVERS AND STREAMS!

Early people also looked to rivers and streams to provide food. We fished and hunted for shellfish and other animals that lived in rivers. We gathered plants that grew in and around rivers. And we hunted for animals, such as birds and deer, that came to rivers and streams for food or water. In fact, today's humans rely on rivers for many of the same things.

Can you imagine a world without rivers and streams? These freshwater bodies are a critical part of the planet's ecosystem! We'll learn more about their role in human history in the next chapter.

 CONSIDER AND DISCUSS

It's time to consider and discuss: What would the world be like without rivers and streams?

PREHISTORIC FISHING

Cave paintings and other ancient **artifacts** provide evidence that humans have been fishing for at least 40,000 years. Cave paintings show fish and other sea creatures. Shellfish **middens** and discarded fish bones show that early humans ate fish. Ancient fish hooks, barbed harpoons, and other fishing equipment give us an idea of how our **ancestors** caught their fish.

 PS You can take a look at some cave paintings in Indonesia at this website!

KEYWORD PROMPTS

cave artists Sulawesi

PROJECT!

EVAPORATING MINERALS

Even though river water isn't salty like ocean water, fresh water does contain low levels of salt and other minerals. One way to extract the salt and minerals from the water is by evaporation.

1 Pour the water and salt into the bowl and mix them together until the salt has completely **dissolved**.

2 Lay the black paper on the baking sheet. Pour the salt **solution** onto the baking sheet, making sure that the water completely covers the paper. Put the baking sheet somewhere warm, such as on a table by a window or outside in the sun.

3 Start a scientific method worksheet in your journal. What do you think will happen in the pan? Check the baking sheet several hours later. Check it again the next day. Write down your observations.

4 Do these steps using the river water you collected in a previous activity. How are your results different? Record your observations and results in your journal.

SUPPLIES

* 1 tablespoon kosher salt
* 2 cups water
* pot or bowl
* spoon
* rimmed baking sheet
* sheet of black construction paper
* science journal and pencil

THINK ABOUT IT! As

the water evaporates, what happens to the saltiness of the water that's left? How would this change in saltiness affect animals or plants that live in a river?

WORDS TO KNOW

mineral: a naturally occurring solid found in rocks and in the ground. Rocks are made of minerals.

dissolve: to mix with a liquid and become part of the liquid.

solution: a mixture of two or more substances, usually a liquid.

21

MAKE A CLOUD

Clouds form when water droplets in the air clump together. One way to encourage this clumping is to give them something to cling to, such as dust or smoke. You can make your own cloud in a bottle this way!

1 At the top of a new page in your science journal, write "Make a Cloud," then make a scientific method worksheet with the following information.

- **Question:** Can I make a cloud in a bottle?

- **Research:** What do you already know about how clouds are formed?

- **Hypothesis/Prediction:** What do you think will happen in the bottle? Will you see a cloud?

2 Heat the water in the pot so that it's hot but not boiling. About 120 to 130 degrees Fahrenheit (49 to 54 degrees Celsius) is right.

3 Using the funnel, pour a small amount of the water into the bottle, just enough to cover the bottom with about a half inch of water.

4 Put the cap on the bottle and swirl the water around so you wet the insides of the bottle. Take off the cap.

PROJECT!

5 Have an adult strike a match and blow it out after a few seconds.

6 Drop the blown-out match into the bottle and immediately put the cap back on the bottle.

7 Squeeze the sides of the bottle hard three or four times. Wait a few seconds and then squeeze again, holding the squeeze longer before you release it. What do you see? Write down your results or draw a picture in your journal.

THINK ABOUT IT! What is happening? How can you explain the results that you see?

PROJECT!

FREEZING POINT

Have you ever wondered why rivers and streams freeze more easily than oceans in the winter? Let's experiment.

1 Use the tape and marker to label one bowl "river" and one bowl "ocean." Put 4 cups of water in each bowl.

2 Add the salt to the "ocean" bowl and stir it until the salt is completely dissolved. Put both bowls in the freezer and leave them for a couple of hours.

3 On a new page in your journal, make a scientific method worksheet by writing the following headings and information.

- **Question:** Does salt keep ocean water from freezing?

- **Research:** Write anything you already know about fresh water and salt water and when they freeze.

- **Hypothesis/Prediction:** Write what you think will happen to the two bowls of water. Will both freeze? If so, will one freeze faster than the other?

4 Check the bowls of water. What happened to the water in each bowl? Use the thermometer to check the temperature of the water in each bowl. Hint: If either bowl of water is completely frozen, let it sit out at room temperature for half an hour and then take the temperature of the melted water. Record your results in your journal.

RIVERS IN STORIES

Almost every **civilization** has stories about rivers or the creatures that live in them. In Greek **mythology**, we find Oceanus, the name of both the great river that encircles the earth and the god who rules over the earth's fresh water. Some of the most famous rivers of Greek myth are the rivers of Hades—the underworld—including the Styx and Lethe, the river of forgetting. Scandinavian folklore has male water spirits called the näcken, which lured women and children into lakes and streams. The bäckahäst—which translates as "brook horse"—is a white horse that appeared near rivers during foggy weather. If someone tried to ride her, they would be unable to get off before she jumped into the river to drown the rider.

Have you read any classic childhood books that take place on or around rivers? How about Kenneth Grahame's *The Wind in the Willows* and Holling Clancy Holling's *Paddle-to-the-Sea*? Can you think of other stories about rivers? Why do you think rivers are fascinating to writers and readers?

TRY THIS! Repeat the experiment by changing the amount of salt in the water. Which bowl freezes and which one remains unfrozen?

CHAPTER 2

HUMANS AND RIVERS AND STREAMS

The history of humanity is tightly connected to rivers and streams. Even if you live nowhere near a stream or river today, your ancestors probably did.

Rivers are sources of fresh water and food for humans. They also provide a way to travel and to transport goods. They make it possible to farm in dry lands. The flow of water can be used as a source of energy. Rivers even give us a place to play.

? INVESTIGATE!

How did early people decide where to live? How is this different from current times?

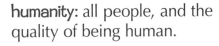

humanity: all people, and the quality of being human.

rapids: sections of a river with fast-moving, turbulent water.

WORDS TO KNOW

EARLY HUMAN MIGRATION

Imagine you lived hundreds of years ago and the place where you lived was getting too crowded or the soil was no longer good for farming. You might have to move. How would you find a new place to live? What would you look for? If you were like our early ancestors, you might follow a river.

Rivers provided early humans with many important things. Rivers were also an efficient way to travel from one area to another, to explore new land, and to trade with other people.

RAPIDS!

When a river flows over a very steep hill or cliff, it forms a waterfall. If the hill is a bit less steep and the river's bed is very rocky, the fast-moving water can form **rapids**. Rapids are sections of the river where the water's flow is fast and turbulent. When the fast-moving water splashes around the rocks, air bubbles get mixed into the water, making the water look foamy and white. Rapids can be very dangerous, but if you have the right equipment and know how to handle it, you can ride the whitewater and feel the river's power for yourself.

RIVERS AND STREAMS!

RIVERS AND FARMING

Rivers played an important role in the development of farming. Large farms require lots of fresh water! Long ago, farmers built their farms near rivers or other sources of fresh water. This way, they could pull water out of the river with buckets and other containers or by digging irrigation ditches from the river into their fields.

Rivers not only provide a source of fresh water to farms, they also help **enrich** the soil in the land around them. Rivers carry **nutrients** in their water in the form of organisms and plants.

SAHARA DESERT RIVERS

Humans first **evolved** in Africa, but why and how did we spread all over the world? Humans probably started leaving Africa around 100,000 years ago. Some scientists think that a major change in the climate in Africa might have encouraged humans to seek new lands by traveling out of Africa. But how did they decide what route to take, and how did they survive traveling across the great Sahara Desert, which today covers most of North Africa? Scientists have discovered that a vast river system used to flow where the desert is now. Migrating humans might have followed the rivers from central Africa and up through the north of Africa.

PS

You can see photographs of where these rivers used to run at this website.

Read about a modern day traveler's journey through Africa.

 KEYWORD PROMPTS

└ — → river Sahara 🔍

 KEYWORD PROMPT

└ — → Out of Eden

WORDS ⊕ KNOW

floodplain: an area of land next to a stream or river that experiences flooding.

BCE: put after a date, BCE stands for Before Common Era and counts down to zero. CE stands for Common Era and counts up from zero. These non-religious terms correspond to BC and AD. This book was printed in 2018 CE.

water wheel: a machine that converts the energy of flowing or falling water into energy that can be used to perform a task, such as grinding wheat into flour.

WORDS ⊕ KNOW

When rivers flood their banks, they spread these nutrients over the soil of the land right next to the river, called the floodplain. Some of the best farming land is found in the floodplain.

RIVERS AND ENERGY

As people became more advanced, they discovered another thing that rivers could provide—energy! By putting a water wheel in the river's current, humans can harness the energy of the river's motion.

DID YOU KNOW?

Mesopotamia, the earliest river valley civilization, rose in the area between the Tigris and Euphrates Rivers beginning around 3500 BCE. Today, this area is modern-day Iraq in western Asia.

RIVERS AND STREAMS!

Early water wheels transferred the water's energy to perform a task on land, such as grinding wheat into flour. In water-powered mills, water from the river flows over or under the water wheel, turning the wheel. Connected to the water wheel is a smaller wheel with **gears**.

This wheel is connected to a still smaller geared wheel, which is attached to a **shaft** that drives the machinery. In a grain mill, this machinery includes the millstones that grind the grain into flour.

Dams are another way humans use rivers. Dams stop or slow the flow of a river. By controlling the flow of a river, a dam can help protect farms or land where people live from flooding. Dams also allow us to move water to places that normally don't have enough water, to be used either for drinking or for farming.

DID YOU KNOW?

Los Angeles, California, transports water from the Sierra Nevada Mountains and rivers that are hundreds of miles from the city to **quench** its population's thirst.

30

Dams have also damaged the ecosystems around them. Many **species** of plants and animals have been harmed as a result of a river being slowed, stopped, or redirected.

In the nineteenth century, people learned how to use dams to capture the energy from a river and store it for later use as electricity. This sort of energy, called **hydroelectricity**, is used all over the world, wherever there are swiftly moving rivers.

WHAT DID ONE ENGINEER SAY TO THE OTHER WHEN THE MILL WHEEL STOPPED TURNING?

Waterwheel we do now?

species: a group of living things that are closely related and can produce young.

hydroelectricity: electricity generated by using the energy of a river's flow.

pollute: to make dirty or contaminate.

sewage: waste products.

pollutant: something that makes the air, water, or soil dirty and damages the environment.

WORDS TO KNOW

MAKING A STINK

One of the biggest ways humans affect rivers is by **polluting** them. Sometimes, people pollute rivers directly by dumping trash, **sewage**, or chemicals into bodies of water. **Pollutants** find their way into the water by other means, too. When water comes back to the earth as precipitation, it flows across the land, meeting up with larger streams and rivers until it finds its way back to the oceans. As the water flows across land, it carries with it some of the chemicals and waste it travels through. These pollutants become part of the river, then part of the ocean, then part of the water cycle, spreading pollution all over our planet.

RIVERS AND STREAMS!

You know what else rivers are good for? Fun! People travel on rivers in boats and canoes, on tubes, and in rafts. Plus, you can do a lot of recreational fishing on a river's edge.

Transportation is another great use of rivers. It's far easier to transport goods and people via a waterway than it is to build a road or a railroad. Many towns and cities have grown up along rivers' edges because people could use the rivers to import and export different items they needed and produced.

Rivers have been a part of human history since early times. We must work to take care of them. In the next chapter, you'll learn about how animals depend on rivers!

? CONSIDER AND DISCUSS

It's time to consider and discuss: How did early people decide where to live? How is this different from current times?

CHIEF JOSEPH DAM ON THE COLUMBIA RIVER IN WASHINGTON STATE IS THE THIRD-LARGEST HYDROELECTRIC POWER PRODUCER IN THE UNITED STATES.
CREDIT: U.S. ARMY CORPS OF ENGINEERS

PROJECT!

RIVER SHAPE POEM

SUPPLIES

* science journal
* pen, pencil, or colored pencils
* watercolor markers (optional)

A shape poem, or concrete poem, looks like the subject of the poem. Can you write a poem about a river that looks like a river? You can see several examples of shape poems at this website.

1 Jot down some notes in your science journal. What do you want to say about a river? Your poem could describe how a river looks, how it behaves, who lives in it, or how rivers make you feel. You can write down words, phrases, or full sentences.

KEYWORD PROMPTS

MsEffie concrete poetry 🔍

2 Write a draft of your poem. Don't worry about the shape right now, but a shorter poem will be easier to fit into a shape later.

3 On another page, draw your shape. Try fitting your poem inside the shape. It's okay if sentences in your poem overlap onto the next line. In fact, it might be fun to find interesting places to break the poem's lines to fit into the shape.

4 Use the colored pencils or markers to decorate your poem and draw the landscape around your river.

TRY THIS! Can you write a watershed shape poem? How many parts would it have?

33

ORIGAMI BOAT

Origami is the Japanese art of folding paper. You can make an origami boat that will really float!

1 Fold the paper in half, left to right, then unfold it.

2 Fold it in half again, top to bottom.

3 With the fold still at the top, fold the left and right corners in so that their edges meet in the middle.

4 Fold the top layer of the bottom strip up. Then, flip the paper over and fold the other bottom strip up. You now have a shape that looks sort of like a hat.

5 Open the hat and then collapse it down again into a diamond shape. Tuck the edges of the folded-up strips under each other to get the paper to be flat.

6 With the diamond shape's open end facing down, fold the bottom corner up to the top. Flip the paper over and do the same thing on the other side. You now have an even smaller hat.

7 Open the hat and collapse it into a diamond shape again.

PROJECT!

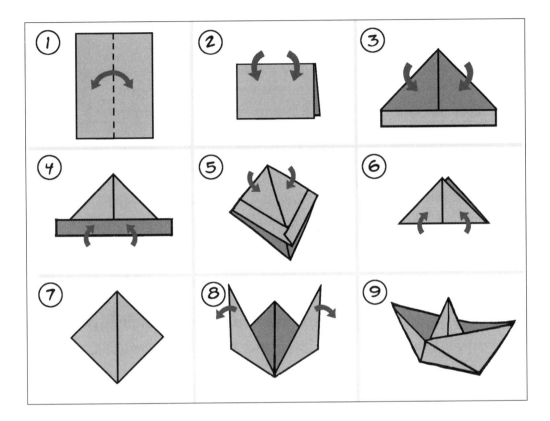

8 Gently pull the top two corners apart and then flatten the shape.

9 Open the sides of your boat, decorate it if you want, and then launch it in the tub, sink, or a nearby stream!

THINK ABOUT IT! How durable is your boat? Does the water make it soggy quickly? How could you make your boat stronger?

PROJECT!

RIVERS AND SETTLEMENTS

Geography affects the shape and path of rivers and streams. How do you think different types of geography and rivers might affect the shape and location of human settlements near them?

SUPPLIES

* science journal and pencil
* drawing paper
* pencils, crayons, or markers

1 Think about the relationship between geography, rivers, and human settlements. For instance, what would a settlement be like if it's near a river that flows through a tight, V-shaped valley?

DID YOU KNOW?

In addition to carrying material goods and food along rivers, our human ancestors also carried their languages, customs, ideas, and diseases. How did all of these things change the communities they traveled through?

What if the river is flowing through a wide, open valley? What if the river has many tributaries or branches? Would a settlement near the source of a river be different from one near the mouth of a river? How?

2 Write your questions and answers in your journal. Draw maps or diagrams to go along with your questions and answers. Did drawing the maps reveal anything that just thinking about the questions didn't?

THINK ABOUT IT! Try asking yourself other questions. What types of plants live near the river? Are there other settlements along the same river? Are there farms, mineral sources, or wildlife? Does the river need to be crossed? How do these factors change how or where the settlement might be built?

WORDS TO KNOW

geography: the features of a place, such as mountains and rivers.

MEASURING A RIVER

SUPPLIES

* piece of paper 8½ by 11 inches
* pens, crayons, or markers
* ruler
* science journal and pencil
* string or twine

It seems as though measuring a river should be easy. To find the width, just measure from one bank to the other. To find the length, start at the source and keep measuring until you reach the mouth. But it turns out that measuring a river is tricky because rivers are always changing their routes, carving new channels, taking shortcuts across curves, and depositing sediment that they've carried for many miles. Any measurement you make of a river is the measurement for only that moment in time. Try measuring a river to see for yourself!

1 Draw a river as a line on your paper. Make it any shape you like, with as many curves and turns as you want. Mark where the source is and where the mouth is.

2 Use the ruler to measure the straight distance from the river's source to the mouth, ignoring the curves. Write down your results in your science journal.

3 Use the ruler to measure the river's length again, but this time measure each segment of the river, from bend to bend. If your river has a few curves in it, you will need to take several measurements. Add the measurements together. Record it in your journal. How does this length compare to the first measurement you took?

TRY THIS! Put the piece of string on the paper and use it to "trace" the river you drew, following all the curves. On the string, mark where the start and end of the river are. Now straighten out the string and measure it with the ruler. How does this length compare to your other measurements?

CHAPTER 3

ANIMALS IN RIVERS AND STREAMS

At first glance, a river might seem like a quiet country road. You might see a few insects hovering, a flock of geese paddling smoothly through the water, or a pair of frog eyes watching you. In reality, healthy rivers are teeming with life!

What sorts of animals live in a river or stream? Many animals that live in the river, such as fish, have adapted to be able to filter oxygen from the water using gills. What other adaptations can you spot in the wildlife around a river or stream?

? INVESTIGATE!

What adaptations have animals made to live in rivers and streams?

FISH

When you think of what lives in rivers and streams, fish are probably the first creatures that come to mind. That's no surprise, because fish are perfectly adapted to the ever-flowing river environment.

Imagine you are walking on a treadmill that has no OFF switch. Life in a river is similar to life on a treadmill. The fish either have to go with the river's flow or they have to continuously swim against the current to keep from being swept away down the river.

Swimming all day against the current takes a lot of energy. To rest, fish find areas of the river where the current is slower, such as a spot protected by large rocks, logs, or a sandbar. Fish also rest in holes in the riverbed.

DID YOU KNOW?

All living beings require salt for their bodies to function. Fish that live in fresh water have evolved to help them retain salt. The gills on freshwater fish trap salt from the water.

invertebrate: an animal without a backbone.

crustacean: a type of animal, such as a crab or lobster, that lives mainly in water. It has several pairs of legs and its body is made up of sections covered in a hard outer shell.

exoskeleton: a skeleton on the outside of a body.

mollusk: an animal with a soft body protected by a shell, such as a clam or snail.

migration: the seasonal movement of animals from one place to another.

WORDS ⊙ KNOW

INVERTEBRATES

Invertebrates are animals that don't have a backbone. **Crustaceans**, like insects, wear their skeletons on the outside of their bodies. This type of skeleton is called an **exoskeleton**. Crayfish and freshwater shrimp are examples of crustaceans that live in rivers and streams.

CRAYFISH

FRESHWATER SHRIMP

Mussels and snails are **mollusks**, which is another group of invertebrates that can be found in rivers. These animals have soft bodies and live in shells.

HOMING SALMON

Salmon are known for their long **migrations** and their ability to live in both salt water and fresh water. After salmon hatch in freshwater streams, they migrate to the ocean and live there for up to five years. When they are mature, they swim back up the river to where they were born to lay their eggs. But how do they know how to find their childhood home? One theory is that they make a mental "map" of their birthplace and then follow that map home.

Some of the tiniest river invertebrates are **microbes**. Microbes include bacteria and **viruses**. These are microscopic creatures! Some microbes become food for larger **aquatic** animals. Others work to break down leaves and other materials in the water into nutrients that are needed by other organisms.

INSECTS

Insects are also invertebrates. Many insects that you see flying around rivers and streams, such as dragonflies, start their lives underwater. The adult insects lay their eggs in the river and the eggs hatch into **larvae**. Insect larvae undergo **metamorphosis** and change into adult insects by shedding their exoskeletons. Some of these adults live on the water, some above the water, and some dive into the water for food!

Some insects help make food for other river dwellers by breaking down dead leaves and plants that fall into the river. And, of course, insects are a favorite food of many other river dwellers, including fish and birds.

microbe: a living thing too small to be seen without a microscope. Also called a microorganism.

virus: a non-living, microscopic particle that can cause disease.

aquatic: living or growing in water.

larva: the worm form of an insect. Plural is larvae.

metamorphosis: an animal's complete change in physical form as it develops into an adult.

WORDS ⊕ KNOW

DID YOU KNOW?

Water beetles dive underwater to find food by taking an air bubble with them so that they can breathe.

AMPHIBIANS

Frogs and salamanders are **amphibians**. Amphibians are **cold-blooded** animals, just like many fish and invertebrates.

Many amphibians start their life in water and then grow up into **terrestrial** adults. For example, some female green frogs lay their eggs in fresh water. The eggs are round and clear, with tiny dark specks in the middle. The dark speck is the **embryo**.

When the eggs hatch, the larvae emerge as **tadpoles**. A tadpole has a tail to help it swim, and gills. Eventually, a tadpole undergoes metamorphosis to become a frog. The gills disappear and the frog's lungs develop fully. The frog now breathes air!

DID YOU KNOW?

The word *amphibious* comes from a Greek word, meaning "living a double life." Can you guess why?

CREDIT: GEOFF GALLICE

predator: an animal that hunts another animal for food.

webbed: having toes or fingers joined by a web or thin covering.

bill: a beak.

absorb: to soak up.

WORDS ⏺ KNOW

BIRDS

The variety of birds that live near rivers and streams is enormous. Rivers and streams provide birds with food, water, shelter, and protection from **predators**.

Waterfowl—which include ducks, geese, and swans—live their entire lives in and around fresh water. They stay warm and dry by grooming their feathers with oil they produce. This makes their feathers waterproof! They have **webbed** feet, which help them swim, and flat **bills**, which help them forage for food in the water.

Wading birds, such as herons and egrets, spend their time on riverbanks, walking on their long legs in the shallow water. They use their sharp beaks to pick fish out of the water and insects and worms out of the mud.

SKIN BREATHERS

Frogs, like most other amphibians, have lungs, but did you know they also breathe through their skin? Amphibians have very thin skin, which allows water and oxygen to pass through it. A few amphibians don't have lungs at all and breathe only through their skin! Many aquatic insects do this, too. But amphibians can't **absorb** oxygen unless their skin is wet, so they must live in moist environments to stay alive.

reptile: a cold-blooded animal such as a snake, lizard, alligator, or turtle, that has a spine, lays eggs, has scales or horny places, and breathes air.

mammal: a type of animal, such as a human, dog, or cat. Mammals are born live, feed milk to their young, and usually have hair or fur covering most of their skin.

WORDS TO KNOW

REPTILES

Reptiles and amphibians seem very similar, but they are distinct groups of animals. Unlike amphibians, reptiles do not have a larval stage and do not undergo metamorphosis. Instead, reptiles lay soft-shelled eggs that hatch into fully developed young. Turtles are reptiles that are commonly found in rivers. Other reptiles include snakes, lizards, tortoises, crocodiles, and alligators.

WHAT IS A FROG'S FAVORITE GAME?

Croak-et!

MAMMALS

Many **mammals** rely on rivers and streams to live. Brown bears regularly visit rivers to hunt for fish. Hippopotamuses—whose name means "river horse"—spend much of the day in shallow rivers and lakes. Beavers are very important river animals. Their dams change the shape of rivers and create habitats for lots of other plants and animals.

Animals aren't the only inhabitants of rivers and streams! In the next chapter, we'll get to know some of the plants that call rivers their home.

CONSIDER AND DISCUSS

It's time to consider and discuss: What adaptations have animals made to live in rivers and streams?

MENTAL MAPS

SUPPLIES

* science journal
* pens, pencils, or markers

Some animals navigate by smell, others by using the position of the sun, and others by sensing the earth's magnetic field the way a compass does. Another way to navigate is to use a mental map. A mental map is a map you carry in your mind. It includes landmarks, such as your house or other buildings, signs, roads, rivers, and other geographic features. How accurate is your mental map?

1 Think of an area or route that you are very familiar with, for example, your neighborhood or the route you take from home to school.

2 From memory, draw a map of that area or route. Include as many landmarks as you can. If you're drawing a route to get from one place to another, include arrows that make it clear what path to take.

3 Ask someone who's familiar with the same area or route to draw their version of the map from their memory—don't let them peek at yours first!

4 Compare the maps. How are they different or the same? What landmarks appear on one but not the other?

THINK ABOUT IT! How are your mental maps different from those of migrating animals? What landmarks do you think animals would find important that you don't?

WORDS TO KNOW

magnetic field: an invisible area (or field) created by a magnet.

navigate: to find your way from one place to another.

PROJECT!

LIGHT REFRACTION

SUPPLIES

* ✳ science journal
* ✳ piece of white paper
* ✳ markers, crayons, or colored pencil
* ✳ clear jar or glass
* ✳ water

When light passes from air to water—or the other way around—the light bends. This is called refraction. Birds that hunt for fish in rivers or fish that hunt for insects on the surface need to know this so they can catch their dinner.

1 Start a scientific method worksheet in your science journal. What do you think will happen when you view a drawing through water?

2 Draw two or more fish on the paper. Draw one above the other and don't make them wider than the jar or glass you are using.

3 Prop your drawing up against a wall or another surface so that you can place the jar in front of it. Put the jar about 6 inches in front of the drawing.

4 While looking at the drawing through the jar, have someone else pour water into the jar. What happens to the fish? Write your observations and conclusions in your journal.

TRY THIS! Does it make a difference how close the water is to the paper? What if the jar is square or round? Does the size of the jar make a difference?

WORDS TO KNOW

refraction: when the direction of light changes.

MAKING GILLS

An animal with gills pulls water through its mouth and then pumps the water out over its gills. The gills extract oxygen from the water as the water passes through the gills. You can create your own gills!

1 Mix the water with the coffee grounds in the measuring cup. Imagine the coffee grounds are the oxygen molecules in the water.

2 Put the filter or paper towel over the top of the glass or jar and secure it with the rubber band. Think of the filter as gills.

3 Start a scientific method worksheet in your science journal. What do you think will happen when you pour the water mixture through the filter? Write your predictions in your journal.

4 Carefully pour the water mixture through the filter and into the glass. What did you observe? If the coffee grounds are the oxygen and the filter is the gills, what's left in the glass? Record your observations and conclusions in your journal.

THINK ABOUT IT! What would happen if the coffee filter had bigger holes? What would this mean for the fish?

SUPPLIES

* science journal
* 2-cup measuring cup or small bowl
* 2 tablespoons of coffee grounds, or rice or dried beans
* 1 cup water
* spoon
* clear drinking glass or jar
* rubber band large enough to fit around the glass
* coffee filter or sheet of paper towel

PROJECT!

WIRE WATER STRIDER

Water striders are insects that walk on the surface of water. You can make your own water strider!

Caution: Ask an adult to help you cut the wire.

1 Cut a 12-inch piece of wire. Bend the piece of wire into a flat design to make your water strider.

2 Fill the bowl or basin with cold water and let it rest until the water's surface is still.

3 Gently place your water strider vertically into the water. What happens?

4 Take the water strider out of the water, shake off any excess water, and wait for the water surface to become still again.

5 Gently place your water strider flat on the surface of the water. What happens?

6 Try placing a paperclip on top of your water strider. How many paperclips can it hold above the water?

THINK ABOUT IT! How can you change the shape of your water strider to hold as many paperclips as possible above the water?

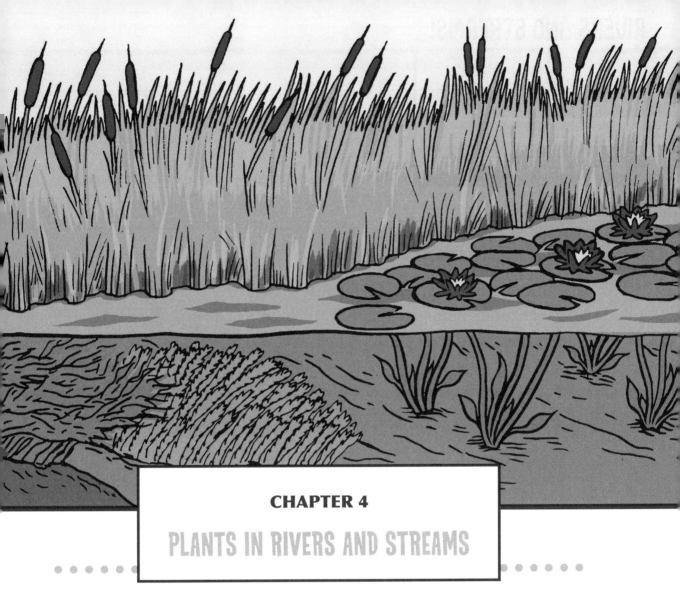

CHAPTER 4

PLANTS IN RIVERS AND STREAMS

Suppose you lived in a river but had no limbs or fins, no lungs or gills, and no way to hold steady or swim against the constantly moving water? How would you survive? How would you raise babies? How would you find food?

Welcome to the life of aquatic plants! Freshwater plants have adapted so that they can grow on riverbanks and above and below a river's surface.

? INVESTIGATE!

What would the world be like without plants?

49

erosion: the wearing away of a surface by wind, water, or other processes.

WORDS to KNOW

Some plants have strong roots that keep them anchored to the riverbed. Others have stems that bend easily with the movement of the water. Some mosses cling to rocks. Water lilies are rooted to the riverbed and have leaves and flowers that float on the surface.

By adapting to river life, aquatic plants help protect humans, animals, the land, and the rivers themselves. They do this by preventing riverbank **erosion**, absorbing pollutants, generating oxygen, and providing animal habitats.

PREVENTING EROSION

Erosion happens when wind, water, and ice wear away soil and rock and move the pieces from one place to another. Riverbank plants are important because they help prevent bank erosion.

RIVERS OF THE WORLD

Geologists estimate a river's age by finding out the age of the mountains the river travels through. By using this method, many scientists believe that the Finke River in Western Australia is the oldest on Earth. This is because the Finke's channel includes several very deep meanders. Since meanders form only on flat land, the river must have formed before the mountains that it now runs through. Those mountains formed around 300 million years ago, which means that the meandering parts of the river existed earlier than that, even before the dinosaurs!

DID YOU KNOW?

Many plants and trees grow along rivers and streams and nowhere else. These plants have adapted to very moist soil or changing levels of moisture in ways that other plants cannot. Wild rice is one type of grass that grows only on freshwater shores.

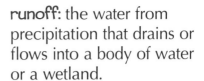

runoff: the water from precipitation that drains or flows into a body of water or a wetland.

wetland: an area where the land is soaked with water, such as a marsh or swamp. Wetlands are often important habitats for fish, plants, and wildlife.

WORDS ⓣⓞ KNOW

When a river's banks erode, the river widens over time. The river becomes shallower and slower, making it less able to whisk storm **runoff** through its channel to drain into larger rivers or lakes. The river is then more likely to flood. Regular flooding is natural and healthy for rivers, but big floods can damage crops, destroy homes, hurt animals, and kill vegetation.

THE EVERGLADES

The Everglades are **wetlands** in Florida that are fed by four rivers. The Everglades contains marshes, which are wetlands that are filled with aquatic grasses of all kinds. The Native Americans who lived in the region, the Seminoles, called the area Pa-hay-Okee, which means "Grassy Waters."

(PS) **Take a video tour of the Everglades at this website.** What animals can you spot? How about plants and trees?

KEYWORD PROMPTS

Everglades tour 🔍

RIVERS AND STREAMS!

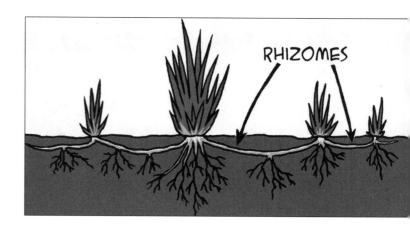

RHIZOMES

Plants that grow along the edges of streams and rivers slow erosion. Reeds and rushes are particularly good at preventing riverbank erosion because they have root systems called rhizomes. Rhizomes grow horizontally away from the plant, under soil or water. Rhizome roots are thick and they act as a kind of net that holds the soil in place.

SPONGING UP POLLUTANTS

Riverbank plants do more than hold soil in place. They also trap sediment and pollutants that run off from the land after a rainstorm. By soaking up pollutants, plants keep harmful toxins out of the freshwater supply.

DID YOU KNOW?

Bamboo, which is native to tropical climates, is another water-loving plant that has a hollow stalk. According to Guinness World Records, the record for the fastest-growing plant belongs to a species of bamboo, which can grow up to 35 inches in a single day!

Mosses are very small, extremely hardy plants that grow everywhere on our planet, from the tops of mountains to shoreline rocks and riverbanks. Mosses do not have roots. Instead, they collect water by absorbing it. To do this, many tiny moss plants grow very close together, forming a **dense**, sponge-like plant that can hold water. This way, they can absorb storm runoff, sediment, and pollutants.

dense: having parts that are very close together.

invasive species: a species that is not native to an ecosystem and that is harmful to the ecosystem in some way.

population: all the people (or plants or animals) in an area or in a group.

WORDS to KNOW

HOME ON THE RIVER

Fertile riverbanks make ideal homes for many species of trees, shrubs, and wildflowers. In turn, these plants provide protection, shade, and food for many animals that call the river home.

WATERMILFOIL

An **invasive species** is one that has no natural predators in its new environment, so the **population** grows at a rapid rate. One example of an invasive species is the Eurasian watermilfoil—an aquatic plant found in many slow-moving rivers, streams, and lakes. Watermilfoil lives well with other plants in its natural environment. But when watermilfoil is transferred to new locations by human activity, it can quickly reproduce. Watermilfoil plants can become so dense they block sunlight from reaching other aquatic plants.

RIVERS AND STREAMS!

Many species of birds, insects, and small animals that come to the river seeking water and food find shelter in the branches and trunks of trees. Some of these animals, and their eggs or offspring, are also food for other animals that come to the river.

HELPING US BREATHE EASIER

Breathe in and thank a plant! Plants generate oxygen as part of **photosynthesis.** During this process, a plant uses water and **carbon dioxide** to change the energy it collects from the sun through its leaves into chemicals that it uses for food. Photosynthesis also produces oxygen, which plants release into the air. Aquatic plants release oxygen into the water, where fish and other aquatic animals can use it.

Some of the tiniest aquatic plants are **phytoplankton.** Phytoplankton are microscopic, free-floating plants that live in both fresh water and salt water. They have no roots, stems, or leaves. Through photosynthesis, they release oxygen into the water, which is used by fish and the rest of us.

WHAT DID THE PLANKTON SAY WHEN IT WAS ASKED HOW THINGS WERE GOING?

"Good, thanks—business is blooming!"

bloom: a rapid increase in the number of plankton or algae.

WORDS ⓉⓄ KNOW

Some studies estimate that phytoplankton produce at least half of the earth's oxygen!

Plants help keep rivers and streams healthy. Without them, aquatic animals could not survive, human life would not exist, and even rivers would be different.

But rivers need more than plants to help keep them flowing. In the next chapter, we'll learn how the relationship between rivers and changing weather patterns affect both rivers and the planet.

?

CONSIDER AND DISCUSS

It's time to consider and discuss: What would the world be like without plants?

PLANKTON BLOOMS

If water has too many nutrients, phytoplankton can grow more quickly than usual and create a blanket across the water. This is called a **bloom.** Some blooms occur naturally and the ecosystems adjusts to them, but others can prevent sunlight from reaching below the water's surface and can cause dead zones. These are areas where there isn't enough oxygen so fish and other organisms cannot survive.

(PS) **Learn about a bloom in the Arctic Sea at this website.**

KEYWORD PROMPTS

Phytoplankton Bloom Arctic video 🔍

PROJECT!

RIVERBANK EROSION

Riverbank plants help hold soil in place and absorb storm runoff and pollutants. See how this works by using kitchen sponges as riverbank plants.

SUPPLIES

* large plastic container or disposable paint tray
* potting soil
* water
* paper cup
* scissors
* kitchen sponges
* science journal and pencil

1 Fill the container halfway with potting soil. Mix the potting soil with about a cup of water so that the soil holds together. You don't want it to be really wet, just enough so you can shape it.

2 Push most of the soil to one side to make a hill that slopes from one end of the container to the other.

3 Use the scissors to poke a hole in the bottom of the paper cup. Hold the paper cup over the top of your hill and then pour about a cup of water into the paper cup. The water will come out of the hole onto the soil. What happens?

BUFFERING

The area near a river covered in **vegetation** is called a **riparian buffer**. Some studies have shown that removing the riparian buffer can cause the water's temperature to rise by as much as 15 degrees Fahrenheit (9 degrees Celsius). That much of a change in water temperature can make it hard for some river plants and animals to survive.

WORDS TO KNOW

vegetation: all the plant life in a particular area.

riparian buffer: the area near a river or stream covered in vegetation.

PROJECT!

EROSION ON THE BANKS OF THE SAÔNE RIVER IN FRANCE

4 If a lot of the soil moved, scrape it back up onto the slope. Arrange the kitchen sponges so they form a line across the container at the top of the hill.

5 Pour water through the paper cup again at the top of the hill. What happened this time?

THINK ABOUT IT! The sponges in this activity are sitting on the surface of the soil. Real plants have roots. Would the results be different if you used real plants on the riverbank? If so, how?

57

PROJECT!

FRACTAL PATTERN WINDOW CLING

A **fractal** is a physical or geometric pattern that **repeats itself in smaller and smaller copies. In nature, we see fractal patterns in many places. River networks are one example. Leaf veins are another. You can make a beautiful piece of art for your window with fractal patterns.**

SUPPLIES

* pen or marker
* piece of paper
* 1-gallon Ziploc bag (or a clear sheet protector)
* bowls
* spoons
* 4 or more tablespoons of white school glue
* 4 or more drops of dish soap
* food coloring
* paintbrushes

1 Use the pen or marker to draw your leaf design on a piece of paper. Draw the outline of the leaf, then draw the repeating fractal pattern of the leaves. Draw a circle or other smooth shape around the outside of the leaf.

2 Put the piece of paper inside the Ziploc bag or the sheet protector. In a bowl, mix 2 tablespoons of glue with 2 drops of dish soap.

3 Paint the glue mixture directly on the plastic. Use your paintbrush to fill the entire design to the edge of the circle. This will be the clear background for your design. Hint: The paint should be thick enough so that it will be sturdy enough to cling to a window, but not too thick or it won't dry. Let this layer dry until it's clear, two or more hours.

4 When the first layer is dry, mix another batch of glue paint, this time with a couple drops of food coloring.

WORDS TO KNOW

fractal: a physical or geometric pattern that repeats itself in smaller and smaller copies.

5 Following your template, paint the leaf shape with the colored glue paint. Let this layer dry.

6 When the second layer is dry, mix another batch of glue paint with a different color. Use this color to paint the fractal veins on the leaf.

7 When all the layers are dry, carefully peel the design off the plastic. Press the smooth side to a clean window.

THINK ABOUT IT! What other fractal designs or repeating patterns have you seen in nature? How about tree limbs? Or snowflakes? Or ferns? Can you think of any others?

BREATHING LEAVES

During photosynthesis, plants use the energy of sunlight to convert carbon dioxide into glucose—a form of sugar that plants use for energy to grow—and into oxygen. While we can't watch a plant breathe, we can do an experiment to see evidence of breathing.

Caution: Make sure you get permission from an adult to cut the leaf!

1 Fill the glass or bowl with water. Put the leaf in the water and put the glass with the leaf in a sunny spot in your house, or outside if the weather is nice.

2 Make a scientific method worksheet in your journal and predict what you will see in an hour.

3 After an hour, look carefully at the edges of the leaf in the glass. What do you see? Record your observations in your journal.

TRY THIS! Leave the leaf in the sunlight for several more hours. Do the bubbles increase or decrease? Take two glasses of water and place a fresh leaf in each one. Place one leaf in a dark area and the other in sunlight for two hours. Do the two leaves produce the same amount of oxygen bubbles?

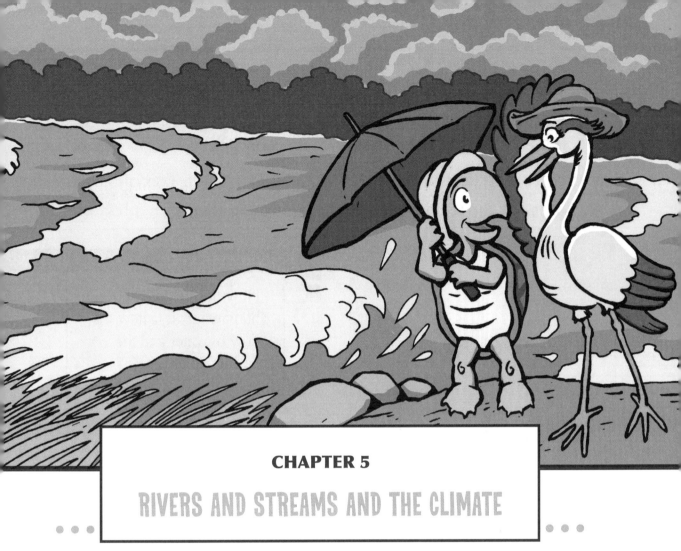

CHAPTER 5

RIVERS AND STREAMS AND THE CLIMATE

Have you heard people talk about climate change? Many people are very concerned about this. Climate is the pattern of weather during long periods of time in a particular location. This includes wind, temperature, and precipitation patterns.

Climate change is partly caused by too much carbon dioxide in the atmosphere. Carbon dioxide can cause the atmosphere to trap too much heat and warm things up on the surface of our planet. This changes our climate in many ways, including warming the water in our oceans, lakes, and rivers.

WORDS TO KNOW

climate change: changes to the average weather patterns in an area during a long period of time.

MODERATING TEMPERATURES

One way that rivers and streams affect climate is by helping to even out the temperature of the air around them.

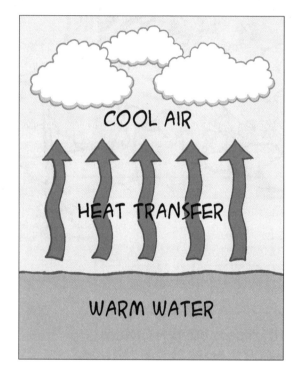

COOL AIR

HEAT TRANSFER

WARM WATER

? INVESTIGATE!

How does nature and human activity affect the flow of water and the landscape?

Heat flows from hotter to colder temperatures. When the air at the water's surface is colder than the water, warmth from the water transfers to the cooler air. This warms the air while cooling the water. When the air is warmer than the water, warmth from the air moves to the water.

This trading of heat between air and water helps even out the temperatures of large bodies of water and the air, making them both more habitable for animals and plants in the area.

DID YOU KNOW?

The year 2016 was the hottest on record, and the temperature of the earth has been rising steadily since the mid 1930s.

RIVERS OF THE WORLD

Rivers are considered sacred bodies of water for many of the world's religions. The Ganges River, which flows through India and Bangladesh, is a holy river to Hindus, who make annual pilgrimages to the river and believe it is good luck to bathe in it, drink its water, or have their ashes scattered in it after their death. The Ganges is the longest river in India and the third largest in the world in terms of water flow. It is used by millions of people. Unfortunately, the Ganges is so well used that it is quite polluted, making the water harmful to humans as well as the fish and animals that depend on the river.

RAINING!

A warmer climate affects many things, including rivers and streams. One reason that a warmer climate changes rivers is related to changes in precipitation.

Warmer air evaporates more water than cooler air does. So, the warmer our climate, the greater the amount of water that is evaporated. This results in more precipitation, but the increased precipitation doesn't fall equally on the planet. Some places get more rain than usual. Other places get much less.

WHAT'S THE DIFFERENCE BETWEEN WEATHER AND CLIMATE?

You can't weather a tree, but you can climate!

Imagine that a river is a hose and its source is a faucet. Most of the time, the faucet is turned on about halfway for a steady flow of water into the hose. If you turn off the faucet, what happens to the water in the hose? What happens if you turn the faucet on all the way?

FAUCET ON HALFWAY

FAUCET ON ALL THE WAY

Changes in precipitation are like changes to the faucet that feeds rivers and streams. A lot less rain or snow means the river's source might dry up or provide much less water. A lot more rain or snow than normal means the river will run much higher than usual.

FLOODING

Water doesn't just evaporate from bodies of water. It evaporates from every surface, including the soil. As soil dries out, it hardens, making it less able to absorb rain quickly. When big storms rain down on dried-out soil, the water floods across the land rather than being absorbed into the soil. When this happens, rivers and streams get more than their usual share of runoff and flood their banks.

Seasonal flooding is a normal part of the water cycle, but intense flooding can cause many problems. Homes and roads can be damaged. Aquatic animals and their eggs can be washed away. And flooding can kill plants that normally thrive on riverbanks.

eon: a very long period of time.

tolerate: to be able to experience something without being harmed by it.

glacier: an enormous mass of frozen snow and ice that moves across the earth's surface.

WORDS ᴛᴏ KNOW

WATER TEMPERATURE

All living things require water to live. Plants and animals—including humans—evolved over **eons** to take the best advantage of the water available to them, no matter where they live on the planet. But when changes to water happen often, or are extreme, we are all less able to cope.

As we've seen, when air temperatures rise, so do water temperatures. This is especially true in relatively shallow bodies of water, such as rivers and streams. Animals, insects, and plants have evolved to **tolerate** normal seasonal changes to water temperature, but bigger changes that last longer can take a toll on river life.

A MISSING RIVER

Scientists blame human-caused climate change for rapid changes to the Slims River in Arctic Canada. The **glacier** that supplied the river with meltwater retreated suddenly in 2016. The Slims, which lost most of its flow because of this change, stopped feeding the lake into which it flowed. Instead, meltwater from the glacier is now flowing into the Gulf of Alaska.

PS Watch a video about this missing river at this website.

KEYWORD PROMPTS

Seeker river missing 🔍

WATER QUALITY

Climate change can also affect how clean and healthy water is. Remember that when rain falls, it falls over land as well as water, flowing across the land to rivers and streams. If the land has many pollutants, the rain carries some of those pollutants into the rivers and streams.

OYSTER-TECTURE

The mouth of the Hudson River, where New York City stands today, was once a **fertile estuary** filled with aquatic life. New York City was once known for its abundance of oysters. In the 1700s, oyster **reefs** were so large they acted as natural protection from storms and flooding. The reefs absorbed energy from waves to break them up and slow them down. But the oysters were over-harvested and the river was polluted. Pretty soon, oysters could no longer thrive in the estuary, and the reefs—along with their storm protection—disappeared. Recently, a design firm has proposed building an artificial oyster reef in the Hudson River, seeding it with baby oysters that will grow into a new reef to help protect the city from future storms.

(PS) **Listen to a podcast about Oyster-tecture at this website.**

KEYWORD PROMPTS
99 Percent Invisible oyster

AN ALGAE BLOOM ON THE RIVER CAM IN ENGLAND   CREDIT: CRUCCONE (CC BY 2.5)

For example, when water flows across fertilized farms and lawns, it carries excess nutrients from the fertilizer into the waterways. When algae in the water feed on these nutrients, it can cause a bloom—a fast increase in the algae population. Algae blooms can produce toxins that are harmful to plants and animals.

In this chapter we've seen how the climate changes rivers and how rivers change the climate. Next, we'll see other ways that rivers are constantly changing, and what we can do to keep rivers and other waterways healthy!

? CONSIDER AND DISCUSS

It's time to consider and discuss: How does nature and human activity affect the flow of water and the landscape?

PROJECT!

WARM WATER AND EVAPORATION

Warm water evaporates more quickly than cold water because the molecules in warm water move more quickly. When they move fast enough, they can jump from the water into the air. We usually can't see molecules without the help of a microscope, but this experiment will help.

SUPPLIES

* ✳ 3 glass jars or large drinking glasses
* ✳ room-temperature water, hot water, cold water
* ✳ science journal and pencil
* ✳ food coloring

Caution: Ask an adult to help you boil the water.

1 Fill one jar with room-temperature water, one with cold water, and one with hot water. For the room-temperature water, fill the jar and leave it on the counter for an hour or two. For the cold water, fill the jar and put it in the refrigerator for an hour or two. For the hot water, have an adult help you boil the water in a kettle or put the jar of water in a microwave oven for a minute or two.

2 In your science journal, make a scientific method worksheet. What do you think will happen when you put food coloring in each jar? Record your predictions in your journal.

3 Put a couple drops of food coloring in each jar. What happens? Record your observations and conclusions in your journal.

THINK ABOUT IT! Since molecules move faster when they are warmer and slower when they are colder, the molecules in the hot water are moving around faster than the molecules in the cold water. The faster molecules mix with the water more quickly, which spreads the color through the water more quickly.

MAKE A THERMOMETER

You can make a simple thermometer to see the changes in air temperature in and around your home.

1 Pour the water and the alcohol into the bottle. Add a couple drops of food coloring to the bottle and swirl the bottle gently to mix in the color.

2 Put the straw in the bottle so that one end is in the liquid but not touching the bottom of the bottle.

3 Wrap the modeling clay around the top of the bottle to hold the straw in place. Be sure not to cover the top of the straw!

4 Observe where the water in the straw is. Try moving the bottle to a location where the temperature is different. When the temperature is warm, the liquid expands and moves up the straw. When the temperature is cool, the liquid contracts and the water moves down the straw.

TRY THIS! If you have a room thermometer, try **calibrating** your thermometer. Find out the current temperature of the air where your thermometer is. Use a marker or piece of tape on the bottle to indicate the current room temperature. Take your thermometer somewhere hotter or colder, measure the air temperature, and then mark the temperature on the bottle.

WORDS ᴛᴏ KNOW

calibrate: to adjust the readings of an instrument and try to get it as accurate as possible.

PROJECT!

MELTING GLACIERS

SUPPLIES

* ice cube tray
* food coloring
* science journal and pencil
* 2 identical plastic containers or a container divided into two sections
* room-temperature water (leave a glass of water on the counter overnight)
* timer

The warming climate causes glaciers to melt faster in the summer than they can refreeze in the winter. When a glacier melts, a river or lake may form at its end. Do you think this water affects how quickly the glacier melts?

1 The day before you do this project, mix a couple drops of food coloring with some water, then put the colored water in an ice cube tray and put it in the freezer.

2 When the ice cubes are frozen, put an equal number of ice cubes in each plastic container. Add a small amount of room-temperature water to one of the containers.

3 In your science journal, make a scientific method worksheet. Which ice cubes do you think will melt more quickly? Record your predictions in your journal.

4 Set the timer. Record the time it takes for the ice in each container to melt. Did the results match your predictions?

THINK ABOUT IT! When ice comes into contact with warmer air or water, it absorbs the surrounding heat. Water is denser than air, so its molecules transfer heat at a faster rate than air does.

CHAPTER 6

HOW RIVERS AND STREAMS ARE CHANGING

A stream of water, as it travels from source to mouth, is always changing, varying with the contours of the land and with the seasons. At the same time, the stream changes the land it runs through.

Outside forces change the river, too. Humans, animals, plants, and the land itself all can change how a river runs. To make sure the planet's rivers stay healthy, practice **conservation** every day!

WORDS TO KNOW

contour: the shape or structure of something.

conservation: the act of managing and protecting natural resources.

71

HUMANS CHANGE RIVERS

Humans build many structures to change rivers to suit our needs. We do this to control flooding, provide drinking water, generate electricity, and transport goods and people.

? INVESTIGATE!

How are healthy streams valuable to people?

One way humans change rivers is by building canals. Canals are artificial waterways that can provide irrigation for farmland or connect large bodies of water together. Dams are another way humans change the course of rivers. Humans have been building dams since before recorded history! Dams are used as part of irrigation systems, to produce drinking water, and to create hydroelectricity. The Hoover Dam is a famous dam in Nevada.

DID YOU KNOW?

There is evidence of Egyptian dams built nearly 5,000 years ago.

oxbow lake: a U-shaped body of water that forms when a meander in a river is cut off.

WORDS ⓣⓞ KNOW

RIVERS OF THE WORLD

The Ucayali River is one of the major tributaries of South American's great waterway: the Amazon River. The Ucayali River runs 907 miles, making it one of the longest rivers in Peru. Many species of animal call the Ucayali home, including several species of fish that live nowhere else in the world. The river is also home to aquatic mammals, including manatees, river dolphins, and giant otters. The native people of Peru first settled near the Ucayali around 2000 BCE. Europeans didn't begin to explore the river until 1806. Like other major rivers, the Ucayali River provides food and many natural resources to the people who live near it, but its most important function is as a means of transportation, acting as a road that connects settlements along its banks and all the way to the Amazon. It's also home to an **oxbow lake**!

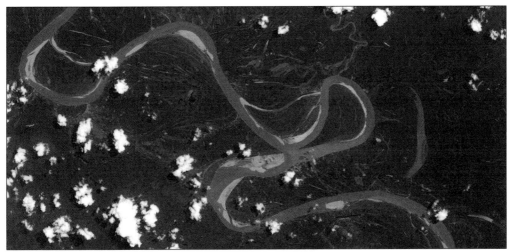

THE UCAYALI RIVER IN PERU WITH THE TOWN HOLANDA   CREDIT: NASA/KJELL LINDGREN

With this animation, you can watch as the course of Peru's Ucayali River changes during the span of 28 years!

KEYWORD PROMPTS

visual news river 🔍

SAVING OUR WATERWAYS

Rivers and streams are incredibly important to life on earth. In turn, we are responsible for helping to keep our rivers and streams healthy. After all, we're all one big ecosystem and rivers rely on us as much as we rely on them.

Everyone can do their part to help keep rivers and streams healthy. Some solutions might seem pretty simple, such as don't pollute! Others might be new to you. Take a look at this list and figure out which actions you can take today to help keep our planet healthy and functioning.

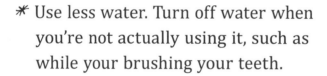

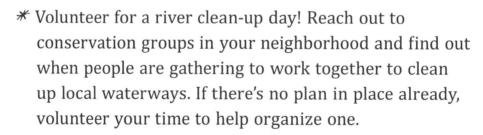

HOW DID THE MONSTERS GET TO THE HALLOWEEN PARTY?

They took the eerie canal!

* Use less water. Turn off water when you're not actually using it, such as while your brushing your teeth.

* Volunteer for a river clean-up day! Reach out to conservation groups in your neighborhood and find out when people are gathering to work together to clean up local waterways. If there's no plan in place already, volunteer your time to help organize one.

* Plant a rain garden near where rain runs off of roads, paths, or driveways. This will help keep runoff from flowing into rivers and streams. Rain gardens are gardens that are slightly below ground level so water can collect there.

✳ Don't flush just anything down the toilet! Cleaning products, medicine, baby wipes—all of these can pollute nearby waterways.

✳ Watch for drips! A few drops of water from a leaky faucet might not seem like a lot, but they can add up to gallons of wasted water.

Taking care of the rivers and streams is an important part of sharing the planet with fellow humans, animals, plants, and even the organisms you can't see! Thanks for helping to keep rivers and streams healthy!

CONSIDER AND DISCUSS

It's time to consider and discuss: How are healthy streams valuable to people?

WOLVES IN YELLOWSTONE PARK

In the mid 1990s, 41 wild wolves were released into Wyoming's Yellowstone National Park to replace the population that had been hunted out of the park. The new wolves thrived, and their population has grown. That one change created a series of other changes in the park, including a decrease in deer population and an increase in vegetation. As this happened, another interesting thing occurred—the rivers changed. With so much more vegetation, there was less erosion along the riverbanks. With more stable banks, the channels narrowed and meandered less. The loss of wolves and then their reintroduction changed the physical geography of rivers in Yellowstone Park!

  You can watch a video about this at this website

KEYWORD PROMPTS

wolf reintroduction Yellowstone 🔍

BUILD A DAM

Can you design and build a dam that keeps water from flooding from one side of the dam to the other?

1 Fill the plastic container about halfway with sand. Dig a path for your river through the sand.

2 Use the popsicle sticks and small rocks to build a dam somewhere across the river.

3 Test your dam by pouring water on one side of the dam. Did any water make it through to the other side?

4 Make changes to your dam until you can keep most of the water on one side of the dam.

TRY THIS! When a dam is built on a river, what happens to the wildlife that depends on the river as a source of food and a place to safely reproduce? Can you think of ways to reduce the impact on the plants and animals that are affected by dams?

THINK ABOUT IT! Rivers have currents. What would happen to your dam if you added a current to your model, such as water from a hose? Would your dam be strong enough to keep the water behind it? What changes would you make to deal with the current and still keep your dam working?

PROJECT!

CANDY EROSION

This quick activity will show you how powerful a force moving water can be.

SUPPLIES

* 3 small jars with tight-fitting lids
* water
* 3 pieces of hard candy
* science journal and pencil

1 Fill the jars halfway full of cool water, put a piece of candy in each jar, and put a lid on each jar.

2 Imagine each piece of candy is a pebble in a body of water. The first candy is in a quiet pond. The second candy is in a slow-moving river. The third candy is in a turbulent stream. In your science journal, start a scientific method worksheet. Predict what will happen to each "pebble."

3 Leave the "pond" jar on the counter. Swirl the "slow river" jar slowly in circles for two minutes. Shake the "turbulent stream" jar for two minutes.

4 Open the jars and compare the pieces of candy. What happened? Record the results and your conclusions.

THINK ABOUT IT! Rocks and pebbles are a lot harder than candy, but the process of erosion is pretty much the same for them as it was for your candy. Imagine how many years it would take for water to erode sharp rocks into smooth pebbles!

RIVER-CROSSING PUZZLE

SUPPLIES

* white paper or colored construction paper
* colored pencils
* scissors

River-crossing puzzles are an ancient challenge, dating back to the ninth century! Wrap your brain around this puzzle and see how long it takes you to solve it.

A farmer uses a little boat to cross the river to go from his farm to the market. At the market, the farmer buys a hen, a bushel of corn, and a bird-hunting dog. The boat is so small that the farmer can carry only one of these things back at a time with him across the river. Can you figure out how the farmer gets everyone across the river safely?

1 Cut out a boat shape from the paper. Cut out shapes to represent the farmer, the hen, the bushel of corn, and the dog. Use the colored construction paper or the colored pencils to make each item different.

2 On a sheet of paper, draw the river the farmer must cross. Place all the shapes on one shore of the river. Use your paper boat and other shapes to solve the puzzle using these rules.

- Only the farmer and one other item are allowed in the boat at the same time.

- If the farmer leaves the hen and the corn together on the shore, the hen will eat the corn.

- If the farmer leaves the dog and the hen alone together, the dog will bite the hen.

3 How many trips does the farmer have to take to get everything safely across the river? You can find the answer on page 88.

PROJECT!

TRY THIS! Once you've figured out the puzzle, try making up your own brainteaser about rivers! Try it on a friend. Can they figure it out?

HOW LOW CAN YOU GO?

The Grand Canyon in Arizona was formed by many natural forces, including erosion by the Colorado River. The Grand Canyon is about 6,000 feet at its deepest. As grand as it is, the Grand Canyon isn't the deepest on Earth. That award goes to the Yarlung Zangbo Grand Canyon in Tibet. The canyon reaches its deepest passage—19,000 feet—when the Yarlung Zangbou River runs through a narrow channel between two mountain peaks.

PREDATOR AND PREY GAME

The re-introduction of wolves into Yellowstone Park had a dramatic effect on the park's ecosystem. This game of foxes and rabbits will give you an idea of the intricate relationship between predators and their prey.

SUPPLIES

* river journal
* 100 pennies or beans (rabbits)
* 10 index cards cut in half to make 20 squares (foxes)
* large table or a clear area on the floor

The rules.

- The first round (generation 1) starts with three rabbits and one fox.

- A fox catches a rabbit when it touches it.

- To survive to the next round, a fox must catch at least three rabbits.

- If a fox doesn't catch three rabbits, the fox dies.

- If a fox captures three or more rabbits, the fox survives and its population doubles in the next round.

- If a rabbit survives, its population doubles in the next round.

1 In your journal, make a chart like the one at the bottom of page 81.

2 Place three coins as your rabbits (prey) in the meadow. Spread them out. In the "Gen 1" column in your chart, write "3" for "# of prey starting," and "1" for "# of predators starting."

3 Toss one predator card (fox) onto the table. Try to make the card land on as many rabbits as possible.

4 Remove any rabbits captured. If the fox didn't catch three rabbits, remove the fox, too.

PROJECT!

5 Count how many rabbits and foxes remain in the meadow and record this in the "# of prey remaining" and "# of predators remaining" boxes for Gen 1.

6 Double the number of remaining rabbits in the meadow. Spread them around evenly. If the fox died, toss one new fox into the meadow. If the fox survived, pick up the surviving fox, then toss double the number of surviving fox cards into the meadow.

7 Remove any rabbits captured and any foxes that didn't survive. Count what's left and record it in the "Gen 2" column of your chart.

8 Repeat this process until you go through 10 generations. What happened to the predator/prey balance as time went by?

	Gen 1	Gen 2	Gen 3	Gen 4	Gen 5	Gen 6	Gen 7	Gen 8	Gen 9	Gen 10
# of prey starting	3									
# of predators starting	1									
# of prey remaining										
# of predators remaining										

THINK ABOUT IT! What do you think would happen if a new predator, such as a wolf, is added to the meadow?

RIVERS AND STREAMS CROSSWORD

Use the words you've learned in this book to complete this crossword puzzle!

DOWN

1 To drop or leave something.
2 The land on the edge of a body of water.
3 The source of a river or stream.
4 A characteristic or distinctive feature of something.
6 The height of something in relation to something else.
7 The path of a river or stream.
8 The movement of water in a river or stream.
10 A stream that flows away from the main channel of a river.
11 The ground that a river flows over.
12 Water from underground that flows up to the surface.

ACROSS

1 Land that forms at a river's mouth.
5 A channel of flowing water, such as river or stream.
9 Where a river or stream's water meets the riverbank.
13 A river's start.
14 An area of land where all the water collects and drains into one body of water.
15 A large stream.
16 A river's end.

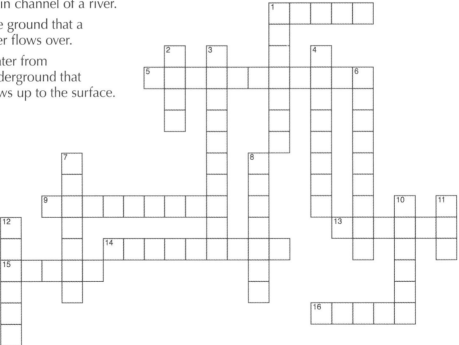

A

absorb: to soak up.

adapt: to make a change to survive in new or different conditions.

algae: a plant-like organism that lives in water and grows by converting energy from the sun into food.

amphibian: an animal with moist skin that is born in water but lives on land. An amphibian changes its body temperature by moving to warmer or cooler places. Frogs, toads, newts, efts, and salamanders are amphibians.

ancestor: someone from your family or culture who lived before you.

aquatic: living or growing in water.

archipelago: a group of islands.

artifact: an object made by people in the past, including tools, pottery, and jewelry.

B

bacteria: tiny organisms that live in animals, plants, soil, and water. Some bacteria are helpful and some are harmful.

bank: the land on the edge of a body of water. Riverbanks are the land on either side of the river's channel.

BCE: put after a date, BCE stands for Before Common Era and counts down to zero. CE stands for Common Era and counts up from zero. These non-religious terms correspond to BC and AD. This book was printed in 2018 CE.

bed: the ground that a river flows over, including the land at the bottom of the river and the sides up to the river's waterline.

bill: a beak.

bloom: a rapid increase in the number of plankton or algae.

branch: a stream that flows away from the main stem of a river.

C

calibrate: to adjust the readings of an instrument and try to get it as accurate as possible.

carbon dioxide: a colorless, odorless gas formed during breathing, burning fossil fuels, and the decay of vegetable matter.

channel: a river or stream's path.

civilization: a community of people that is advanced in art, science, and government.

climate: the average weather patterns in an area during a long period of time.

climate change: changes to the average weather patterns in an area during a long period of time.

cold-blooded: animals that cannot produce their own heat, so their body temperature is the same as the air around them.

condensation: when water vapor turns into a liquid.

conservation: the act of managing and protecting natural resources.

contour: the shape or structure of something.

creek: a small stream, also called a brook. The word you use for this depends on where you live. For example, some people call a small stream a creek, a kill, or a run.

crustacean: a type of animal, such as a crab or lobster, that lives mainly in water. It has several pairs of legs and its body is made up of sections covered in a hard outer shell.

current: the movement of the water in a body of water. In rivers and streams, the current moves in one direction: downhill toward the ocean.

D

dam: a barrier constructed across a waterway that helps control the water flowing behind it.

delta: land that forms from the buildup of sediment carried by a river to its mouth.

dense: having parts that are very close together.

deposit: to drop or leave something.

dissolve: to mix with a liquid and become part of the liquid.

E

ecosystem: a community of plants and animals living in an area, relying on each other to survive.

elevation: the height of something above sea level.

embryo: an organism at its early stages of development.

enrich: to improve soil quality by adding nutrients to it.

eon: a very long period of time.

equator: the imaginary line around the earth, halfway between the North and South Poles.

erosion: the wearing away of a surface by wind, water, or other processes.

estuary: the area at the mouth of a large river where it meets the ocean tide.

evaporation: the process by which a liquid becomes a gas.

evolve: to gradually develop through time and become more complex.

exoskeleton: a skeleton on the outside of a body.

export: to send goods to another country to sell.

F

fertile: land and water that is good for growing plants and other organisms.

flooding: when water covers an area that is usually dry.

floodplain: an area of land next to a stream or river that experiences flooding.

fractal: a physical or geometric pattern that repeats itself in smaller and smaller copies.

G

gear: a wheel with teeth that fits around another wheel with teeth so that energy can be transmitted from one to the other.

geography: the features of a place, such as mountains and rivers.

gills

gills: filter-like structures that let an organism get oxygen out of the water to breathe.

glacier: an enormous mass of frozen snow and ice that moves across the earth's surface.

H

habitat: an area where certain plants and animals live together.

headwaters: the source of a river or stream.

humanity: all people, and the quality of being human.

hydroelectricity: electricity generated by using the energy of a river's flow.

I

import: to bring in goods from another country to sell.

inhabitant: a person, animal, or other organism that lives in a particular place.

invasive species: a species that is not native to an ecosystem and that is harmful to the ecosystem in some way.

invertebrate: an animal without a backbone.

irrigation: the process of delivering water to plants or fields where crops are planted.

L

larva: the worm form of an insect. Plural is larvae.

M

magnetic field: an invisible area (or field) created by a magnet.

mammal: a type of animal, such as a human, dog, or cat. Mammals are born live, feed milk to their young, and usually have hair or fur covering most of their skin.

meander: a winding path taken by a stream or river.

metamorphosis: an animal's complete change in physical form as it develops into an adult.

microbe: a living thing too small to be seen with a microscope. Also called a microorganism.

microscopic: something so small it can be seen only with a microscope.

midden: an ancient garbage heap.

migration: the seasonal movement of animals from one place to another.

molecule: a group of atoms, which are the smallest particles of matter.

mollusk: an animal with a soft body protected by a shell, such as a clam or snail.

monsoon: a seasonal wind that often brings seasonal rain.

mouth: the end of a river. The mouth is where the river joins a larger body of water, such as a lake or ocean.

mythology: a collection of stories that are often focused on historical events. Myths express the beliefs and values of a group of people.

N

navigate: to find your way from one place to another.

nutrients: substances in food and soil that living things need to live and grow.

O

organism: a living thing, such as an animal or a plant.

oxbow lake: a U-shaped body of water that forms when a meander in a river is cut off.

P

photosynthesis: the process plants use to turn sunlight, carbon dioxide, and water into food.

phytoplankton: microscopic, drifting plants, such as algae, that live in both fresh water and salt water.

pollutant: something that makes the air, water, or soil dirty and damages the environment.

pollute: to make dirty or contaminate.

population: all the people (or plants or animals) in an area or in a group.

precipitation: the falling to the earth of rain, snow, or any form of water.

predator: an animal that hunts another animal for food.

property: a characteristic, quality, or distinctive feature of something.

Q

quench: to put out a fire or satisfy a thirst.

R

rapids: sections of a river with fast-moving, turbulent water.

reef: an underwater structure made of corals, sand, and rock.

refraction: when the direction of light changes.

reptile: a cold-blooded animal such as a snake, lizard, alligator, or turtle, that has a spine, lays eggs, has scales or horny places, and breathes air.

resource: something that people can use.

rhizome: a horizontal, underground, or underwater plant stem that sends out vertical roots.

riparian buffer: the area near a river or stream covered in vegetation.

river: a large quantity of water that flows through a channel from its source to its mouth.

runoff: the water from precipitation that drains or flows into a body of water or a wetland.

S

sediment: particles of natural material, such as sand or silt, that are carried from one place to another.

sewage: waste products.

shaft: a bar that connects one gear to another and transfers power from one to the other.

solution: a mixture of two or more substances, usually a liquid.

source: where a river or stream starts.

species: a group of living things that are closely related and can produce young.

spring: a place where water from underground flows up to the earth's surface.

stream: a narrow flow of water that has a current that runs in one direction. A river is a type of stream.

T

tadpole: the larval stage of an amphibian.

terrestrial: relating to the earth or soil.

tide: the twice daily rising and falling of ocean water.

tolerate: to be able to experience something without being harmed by it.

toxin: a poisonous or harmful substance.

tributary: a river or stream that flows into a larger river or lake.

tropical: the hot climate zone to the north and south of the equator.

turbulent: being in a state of agitation, or unpredictable motion.

V

vapor: a gas.

vegetation: all the plant life in a particular area.

virus: a non-living, microscopic particle that can cause disease.

W

water cycle: the continuous movement of water from the earth to the clouds and back again.

waterline: the line where a river or stream's water meets the riverbank.

watershed: an area where all the water in an area drains into one river or lake.

waterway: a channel or body of water.

water wheel: a machine that converts the energy of flowing or falling water into energy that can be used to perform a task, such as milling wheat.

webbed: having toes or fingers joined by a web or thin covering.

wetland: an area where the land is soaked with water, such as a marsh or swamp. Wetlands are often important habitats for fish, plants, and wildlife.

METRIC CONVERSIONS

Use this chart to find the metric equivalents to the English measurements in this book. If you need to know a half measurement, divide by two. If you need to know twice the measurement, multiply by two. How do you find a quarter measurement? How do you find three times the measurement?

English	Metric
1 inch	2.5 centimeters
1 foot	30.5 centimeters
1 yard	0.9 meter
1 mile	1.6 kilometers
1 pound	0.5 kilogram
1 teaspoon	5 milliliters
1 tablespoon	15 milliliters
1 cup	237 milliliters

BOOKS

Fiction

Williamson, Henry. *Tarka the Otter*. Penguin Modern Classics, 2009.

Cherry, Lynn. *A River Ran Wild*. HMH Books for Young Readers, 2002.

Holling, Holling Clancy. *Paddle-to-the-Sea*. Sandpiper Books, 1980.

Nonfiction

Schneider, Herman and Nina. *Rocks, Rivers, and the Changing Earth: A First Book About Geology*. Dover Publications, 2014.

Edom, Helen. *Science with Water*. Usborne Pub Ltd., 2007.

Hiscock, Bruce. *The Big Rivers: The Missouri, the Mississippi, and the Ohio*. Atheneum, 1997.

Lauber, Patricia. *Flood: Wrestling with the Mississippi*. National Geographic Society, 1996.

Poetry

National Geographic Book of Nature Poetry. National Geographic Children's Books, 2015.

Yolen, Jane. *Water Music*. WordSong, 2003.

Levy, Constance. *Splash! Poems of Our Watery World*. Orchard, 2002.

WEBSITES

The Man Who Planted Trees: A film of the book by Jean Giono
youtube.com/watch?v=KTvYh8ar3tc

The Mighty River That Dried Up "I am Red":
A brief film about the Colorado River
video.nationalgeographic.com/video/short-film-showcase/
the-mighty-river-that-dried-up-i-am-red

The Life Cycle of the Atlantic Salmon:
An animated video about the life of Scottish Atlantic salmon
youtube.com/watch?v=2fGLzEvWuYA

How to Make a Water Wheel: youtube.com/watch?v=4Bt3psl_ge8

OTHER COOL STUFF

Map of the Rivers of Wales: imgur.com/bWLeGfT

The Lost Rivers of London: bbc.com/news/uk-england-london-29551351

Map of the Words Used for Streams in the United States:
derekwatkins.wordpress.com/2011/07/25/generic-stream-terms

QR CODE GLOSSARY

Page 6: youtube.com/watch?v=yPk7fPpAhXM

Page 20: aramcoworld.com/en-US/Articles/May-2015/Cave-Artists-of-Sulawesi

Page 28: ecowatch.com/ancient-river-system-flowed-under-sahara-desert-it-would-rank-12th-lar-1882118676.html

Page 28: nationalgeographic.org/projects/out-of-eden-walk

Page 33: mseffie.com/assignments/poem-a-day/10.html

Page 51: youtube.com/watch?v=LkNEBAZq0rM

Page 55: youtube.com/watch?v=cpUf2EAmHxk

Page 65: youtube.com/watch?v=s42dVrSoyQc

Page 66: 99percentinvisible.org/episode/oyster-tecture

Page 73: vox.com/2015/2/5/7986829/river-meander

Page 75: yellowstonepark.com/things-to-do/wolf-reintroduction-changes-ecosystem

ESSENTIAL QUESTIONS

Introduction: How would you describe a river to someone who has never seen one before?

Chapter 1: What would the world be like without rivers and streams?

Chapter 2: How did early people decide where to live? How is this different from current times?

Chapter 3: What adaptations have animals made to live in rivers and streams?

Chapter 4: What would the world be like without plants?

Chapter 5: How does nature and human activity affect the flow of water and the landscape?

Chapter 6: How are healthy streams valuable to people?

RIVER-CROSSING PUZZLE

Trip 1: Farmer and hen cross the river, leaving the dog and the corn behind.

Trip 2: Farmer returns alone.

Trip 3: Farmer and dog cross. Farmer puts the dog on the shore and puts the hen in the boat.

Trip 4: Farmer and hen cross. Farmer puts the hen on the shore and puts the corn in the boat.

Trip 5: Farmer and corn cross. Farmer puts the corn on the shore with the dog.

Trip 6: Farmer returns alone.

Trip 7: Farmer puts the hen in the boat and crosses. Everyone is now on the far shore.

CROSSWORD

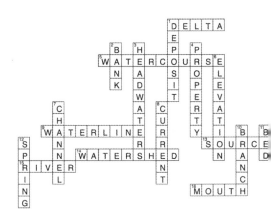